M000222867

To

_____

From

_____

Occasion

_____

a bouquet of

Favorite Psalms

to inspire your soul

Tyndale House Publishers, Inc.

CAROL STREAM, ILLINOIS

Make thankfulness your sacrifice to God,
and keep the vows you made to the Most
High. Then call on me when you are in
trouble, and I will rescue you, and you
will give me glory. . . . Giving thanks is
a sacrifice that truly honors me. If you
keep to my path, I will reveal to you
the salvation of God.

PSALM 50:14-15, 23

Show me the right
path, O LORD;
*point out the road
for me to follow.*

PSALM 25:4

As the deer longs
for streams of water,
so I long for you,
O God.

PSALM 42:1

The LORD is compassionate and merciful, slow to get angry and filled with unfailing love. . . . For his unfailing love toward those who fear him is as great as the height of the heavens above the earth. He has removed our sins as far from us as the east is from the west.

PSALM 103:8, 11-12

How precious . . . are Your thoughts to me,
O God! How great is the sum of them! If
I should count them, they would be more
in number than the sand. . . . Search me,
O God, and know my heart: try me, and
know my anxieties: and see if there is any
wicked way in me, and lead me in the way
everlasting.

PSALM 139:17-18, 23-24, NKJV

BLESSED BE THE NAME
OF THE LORD NOW
AND FOREVER....
HIS GLORY IS HIGHER
THAN THE HEAVENS.

PSALM 113:2,4

I WAITED

patiently

FOR THE LORD;
AND HE INCLINED TO ME,
AND HEARD MY CRY.

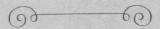

PSALM 40:1, NKJV

Hear my cry, O God; attend unto my prayer. From the end of the earth will I cry unto thee, when my heart is overwhelmed: lead me to the rock that is higher than I. For thou hast been a shelter for me, and a strong tower from the enemy. I will abide in thy tabernacle for ever: I will trust in the covert of thy wings.

PSALM 61:1-4, KJV

The LORD is my shepherd; I have all that I need. He lets me rest in green meadows; he leads me beside peaceful streams. He renews my strength. He guides me along right paths, bringing honor to his name. Even when I walk through the darkest valley, I will not be afraid, for you are close beside me. Your rod and your staff protect and comfort me.

PSALM 23:1-4

THE HEAVENS DECLARE THE GLORY OF GOD;

the skies proclaim the work of his hands.

PSALM 19:1, NIV

Teach me to do your will,
for you are my God.
May your gracious
Spirit lead me forward
on a firm footing.

PSALM 143:10

The LORD directs the steps of the godly.
He delights in every detail of their lives.
Though they stumble, they will never fall,
for the LORD holds them by the hand. . . .
Put your hope in the LORD. Travel steadily
along his path. He will honor you by giving
you the land.

PSALM 37:23-24, 34

How can a young man cleanse his way?
By taking heed according to Your word.
With my whole heart I have sought
You; oh, let me not wander from Your
commandments! Your word I have hidden
in my heart, that I might not sin
against You.

PSALM 119:9-11, NKJV

Before the mountains were
brought forth, or ever you had formed
the earth and the world,

*from everlasting
to everlasting
you are God.*

PSALM 90:2, ESV

The LORD says,
"I will guide you along the best pathway for your life.

I will advise you and watch over you."

PSALM 32:8

As for me, I will sing about your power.
Each morning I will sing with joy about
your unfailing love. For you have been
my refuge, a place of safety when I am
in distress. O my Strength, to you I sing
praises, for you, O God, are my refuge, the
God who shows me unfailing love.

PSALM 59:16-17

All you who
fear the LORD,
trust the LORD!
*He is your helper
and your shield.*

PSALM 115:11

This is the day which
the LORD hath made;
we will rejoice and
be glad in it.

PSALM 118:24, KJV

Enter his gates with thanksgiving; go into his courts with praise. Give thanks to him and praise his name. For the LORD is good. His unfailing love continues forever, and his faithfulness continues to each generation.

PSALM 100:4-5

May the glory of the LORD endure forever;
may the LORD rejoice in his works. . . . I will
sing to the LORD as long as I live; I will
sing praise to my God while I have being.
May my meditation be pleasing to him, for
I rejoice in the LORD.

PSALM 104:31, 33-34, ESV

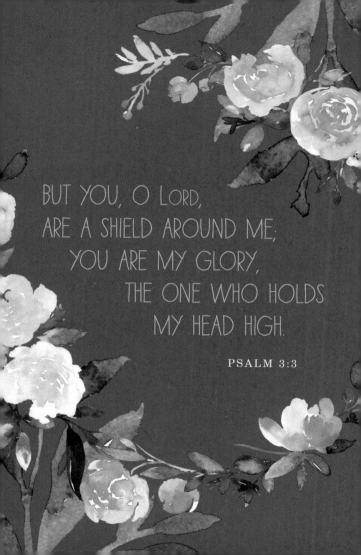

BUT YOU, O LORD,
ARE A SHIELD AROUND ME;
YOU ARE MY GLORY,
THE ONE WHO HOLDS
MY HEAD HIGH.

PSALM 3:3

FOR THIS GOD IS OUR GOD
FOR EVER AND EVER;
HE WILL BE

our guide

EVEN TO THE END.

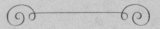

PSALM 48:14, NIV

Make a joyful shout to the LORD, all you lands! Serve the LORD with gladness; come before His presence with singing. Know that the LORD, He is God; it is He who has made us, and not we ourselves; we are His people and the sheep of His pasture.

PSALM 100:1-3, NKJV

Give thanks to the LORD, for he is good!
His faithful love endures forever. Give
thanks to the God of gods. His faithful love
endures forever. Give thanks to the Lord
of lords. His faithful love endures forever.
Give thanks to him who alone does mighty
miracles. His faithful love endures forever.

PSALM 136:1-4

I WAIT FOR
THE Lord, MY WHOLE
BEING WAITS,
and in his word
I put my hope.

PSALM 130:5, NIV

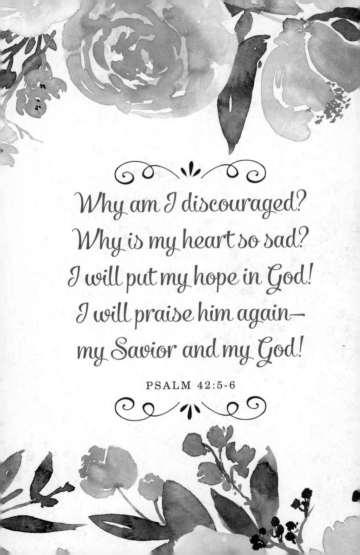

Why am I discouraged?
Why is my heart so sad?
I will put my hope in God!
I will praise him again—
my Savior and my God!

PSALM 42:5-6

O Lord, you have examined my heart and know everything about me. You know when I sit down or stand up. You know my thoughts. . . . You know everything I do. You know what I am going to say even before I say it, Lord. You go before me and follow me. You place your hand of blessing on my head.

PSALM 139:1-5

Make haste, O God, to deliver me; make haste to help me, O LORD. . . . But I am poor and needy: make haste unto me, O God: thou art my help and my deliverer; O LORD, make no tarrying.

PSALM 70:1, 5, KJV

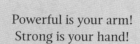

Powerful is your arm!
Strong is your hand!

*Your right hand
is lifted high in
glorious strength.*

PSALM 89:13

O LORD,
hear my
plea for
justice.
Listen to my
cry for help.

Pay attention to my prayer, for it comes from honest lips.

PSALM 17:1

Bless the LORD, O my soul! O LORD my God,
you are very great! You are clothed with
splendor and majesty, covering yourself
with light as with a garment, stretching out
the heavens like a tent. . . . He makes the
clouds his chariot; he rides on the wings of
the wind.

PSALM 104:1-3, ESV

But you, O LORD,
will sit on your
throne forever.
Your fame will
endure to every
generation.

PSALM 102:12

Your love, LORD,
reaches to the heavens,
your faithfulness
to the skies.

PSALM 36:5, NIV

Praise the LORD! Praise God in his sanctuary; praise him in his mighty heaven! Praise him for his mighty works; praise his unequaled greatness! . . . Praise him with the lyre and harp! Praise him with the tambourine and dancing; praise him with strings and flutes! Praise him with a clash of cymbals. . . . Let everything that breathes sing praises to the LORD! Praise the LORD!

PSALM 150:1-6

I will call on God, and the LORD will rescue me. Morning, noon, and night I cry out in my distress, and the LORD hears my voice. He ransoms me and keeps me safe from the battle waged against me, though many still oppose me. God, who has ruled forever, will hear me and humble them.

PSALM 55:16-19

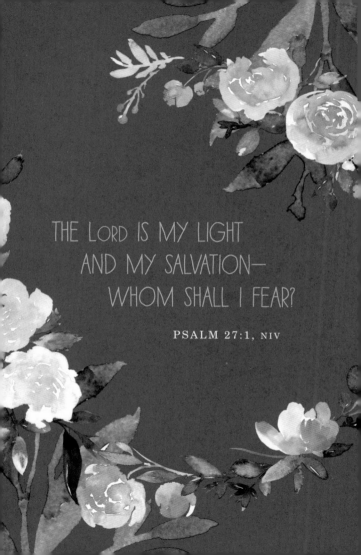

THE Lord IS MY LIGHT
AND MY SALVATION—
WHOM SHALL I FEAR?

PSALM 27:1, NIV

PRAISE THE LORD;

praise

GOD OUR SAVIOR!
FOR EACH DAY HE CARRIES
US IN HIS ARMS.

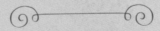

PSALM 68:19

"I will remember the deeds of the LORD; yes, I will remember your miracles of long ago. I will consider all your works and meditate on all your mighty deeds." Your ways, God, are holy. What god is as great as our God? You are the God who performs miracles; you display your power among the peoples. With your mighty arm you redeemed your people.

PSALM 77:11-15, NIV

Praise the LORD, my soul; all my inmost being, praise his holy name. Praise the LORD, my soul, and forget not all his benefits—who forgives all your sins and heals all your diseases, who redeems your life from the pit and crowns you with love and compassion, who satisfies your desires with good things so that your youth is renewed like the eagle's.

PSALM 103:1-5, NIV

WE THANK YOU,
O GOD! WE GIVE
THANKS BECAUSE
YOU ARE NEAR.

*People everywhere tell
of your wonderful deeds.*

PSALM 75:1

Come, everyone!
Clap your hands!
Shout to God with joyful
praise! For the LORD
Most High is awesome.

PSALM 47:1-2

Long ago you laid the foundation of the earth and made the heavens with your hands. They will perish, but you remain forever; they will wear out like old clothing. You will change them like a garment and discard them. But you are always the same; you will live forever.

PSALM 102:25-27

The LORD of hosts is with us; the God of Jacob is our refuge. Come, behold the works of the LORD, who has made desolations in the earth. He makes wars cease to the end of the earth; He breaks the bow and cuts the spear in two; He burns the chariot in the fire.

PSALM 46:7-9, NKJV

Because of your unfailing love,
I can enter your house;

*I will worship
at your
Temple with
deepest awe.*

PSALM 5:7

Who are those who
fear the LORD?

*He will
show them*

the path
they should
choose.

PSALM 25:12

The LORD is in his holy Temple; the LORD
still rules from heaven. He watches everyone
closely, examining every person on earth.
The LORD examines both the righteous
and the wicked. He hates those who love
violence. . . . For the righteous LORD loves
justice. The virtuous will see his face.

PSALM 11:4-5, 7

Sing for joy to God
our strength;
*shout aloud to the
God of Jacob!*

PSALM 81:1, NIV

Joyful are people of
integrity, who follow
the instructions
of the LORD.

PSALM 119:1

Out of the depths I cry to you, LORD; Lord, hear my voice. Let your ears be attentive to my cry for mercy. If you, LORD, kept a record of sins, Lord, who could stand? But with you there is forgiveness, so that we can, with reverence, serve you.

PSALM 130:1-4, NIV

Oh, the joys of those who do not follow
the advice of the wicked, or stand around
with sinners, or join in with mockers.
But they delight in the law of the LORD,
meditating on it day and night. They are
like trees planted along the riverbank,
bearing fruit each season. Their leaves
never wither, and they prosper in all
they do.

PSALM 1:1-3

RETURN, O LORD,
AND RESCUE ME. SAVE ME
BECAUSE OF YOUR
UNFAILING LOVE.

PSALM 6:4

LORD, YOU HAVE BEEN OUR

dwelling

PLACE THROUGHOUT
ALL GENERATIONS.

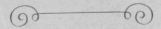

PSALM 90:1, NIV

Unto thee, O LORD, do I lift up my soul.
O my God, I trust in thee: let me not be
ashamed, let not mine enemies triumph
over me. . . . Lead me in thy truth, and
teach me: for thou art the God of my
salvation; on thee do I wait all the day.

PSALM 25:1-2, 5, KJV

O God, you are my God; I earnestly search for you. My soul thirsts for you; my whole body longs for you in this parched and weary land where there is no water. I have seen you in your sanctuary and gazed upon your power and glory. Your unfailing love is better than life itself; how I praise you!

PSALM 63:1-3

O SING UNTO THE
LORD A NEW SONG;
*for he hath done
marvellous things.*

PSALM 98:1, KJV

My help comes from
the LORD, who made
heaven and earth.

PSALM 121:2, ESV

Praise be to you, LORD; teach me your decrees. With my lips I recount all the laws that come from your mouth. I rejoice in following your statutes as one rejoices in great riches. I meditate on your precepts and consider your ways. I delight in your decrees; I will not neglect your word.

PSALM 119:12-16, NIV

God is honored in Judah; his name is great in Israel. Jerusalem is where he lives; Mount Zion is his home. There he has broken the fiery arrows of the enemy, the shields and swords and weapons of war.

PSALM 76:1-3

I praise you because I am
fearfully and wonderfully made;

*your works are
wonderful, I know
that full well.*

PSALM 139:14, NIV

Wake up, lyre and harp! I will wake the dawn with my song.

I will thank you, LORD, among all the people.

PSALM 108:2-3

Have mercy on me, O God, because of your unfailing love. Because of your great compassion, blot out the stain of my sins. Wash me clean from my guilt. Purify me from my sin. For I recognize my rebellion; it haunts me day and night. . . . Purify me from my sins, and I will be clean; wash me, and I will be whiter than snow.

PSALM 51:1-3, 7

Oh, taste and see that the LORD is good; *blessed is the man who trusts in Him!*

PSALM 34:8, NKJV

Forever, O LORD,
Your word is settled
in heaven. Your
faithfulness endures
to all generations.

PSALM 119:89-90, NKJV

The LORD is king forever and ever! The godless nations will vanish from the land. LORD, you know the hopes of the helpless. Surely you will hear their cries and comfort them. You will bring justice to the orphans and the oppressed, so mere people can no longer terrify them.

PSALM 10:16-18

The righteous cry out, and the LORD hears them; he delivers them from all their troubles. The LORD is close to the brokenhearted and saves those who are crushed in spirit. The righteous person may have many troubles, but the LORD delivers him from them all.

PSALM 34:17-19, NIV

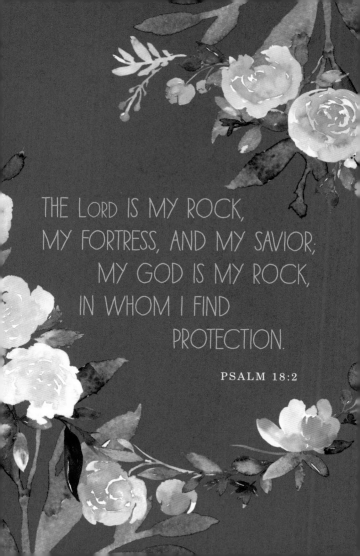

THE LORD IS MY ROCK,
MY FORTRESS, AND MY SAVIOR;
MY GOD IS MY ROCK,
IN WHOM I FIND
PROTECTION.

PSALM 18:2

BETTER IS

one day

IN YOUR COURTS THAN
A THOUSAND ELSEWHERE.

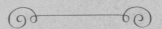

PSALM 84:10, NIV

The LORD is my strength and my song; he has given me victory. Songs of joy and victory are sung in the camp of the godly. The strong right arm of the LORD has done glorious things! The strong right arm of the LORD is raised in triumph. The strong right arm of the LORD has done glorious things!

PSALM 118:14-16

O Lord, open my lips, and my mouth shall show forth Your praise. For You do not desire sacrifice, or else I would give it; You do not delight in burnt offering. The sacrifices of God are a broken spirit, a broken and a contrite heart—these, O God, You will not despise.

PSALM 51:15-17, NKJV

THE LORD GIVES HIS PEOPLE STRENGTH.

The LORD blesses them with peace.

PSALM 29:11

I trust in your unfailing love. I will rejoice because you have rescued me.

PSALM 13:5

O Lord, you alone are my hope. I've trusted
you, O Lord, from childhood. Yes, you have
been with me from birth; from my mother's
womb you have cared for me. No wonder
I am always praising you! My life is an
example to many, because you have been
my strength and protection. That is why I
can never stop praising you; I declare your
glory all day long.

PSALM 71:5-8

My heart is not proud, LORD, my eyes are not haughty; I do not concern myself with great matters or things too wonderful for me. But I have calmed and quieted myself, I am like a weaned child with its mother; like a weaned child I am content.

PSALM 131:1-2, NIV

Unless the LORD
builds the house,

*those who
build it labor
in vain.*

PSALM 127:1, ESV

Praise
God, who
did not ignore
my prayer or

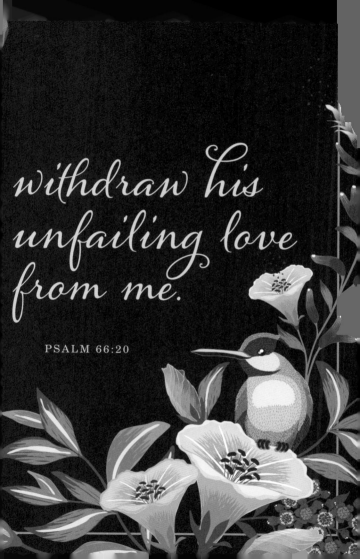

withdraw his unfailing love from me.

PSALM 66:20

Blessed are those whose help is the God of Jacob, whose hope is in the LORD their God. He is the Maker of heaven and earth, the sea, and everything in them—he remains faithful forever.

PSALM 146:5-6, NIV

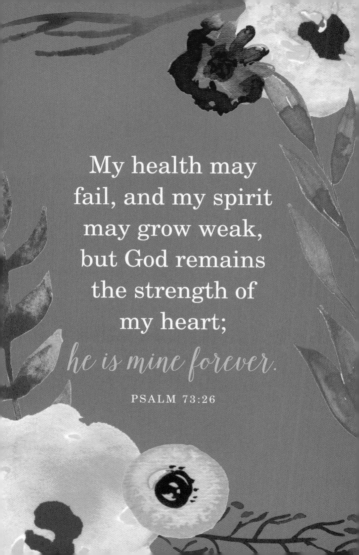

My health may fail, and my spirit may grow weak, but God remains the strength of my heart; *he is mine forever.*

PSALM 73:26

I was glad when
they said to me,
"Let us go to the
house of the LORD."

PSALM 122:1

He upholds the cause of the oppressed and gives food to the hungry. The LORD sets prisoners free, the LORD gives sight to the blind, the LORD lifts up those who are bowed down, the LORD loves the righteous.

PSALM 146:7-8, NIV

The LORD watches over the foreigner and sustains the fatherless and the widow, but he frustrates the ways of the wicked. The LORD reigns forever, your God, O Zion, for all generations. Praise the LORD.

PSALM 146:9-10, NIV

GOD IS MY SHIELD,
SAVING THOSE WHOSE HEARTS
ARE TRUE AND RIGHT.

PSALM 7:10

YOUR RIGHTEOUSNESS,
GOD, REACHES TO
the heavens,
YOU WHO HAVE
DONE GREAT THINGS.
WHO IS LIKE YOU, GOD?

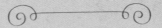

PSALM 71:19, NIV

Blessed is the one who considers the poor! In the day of trouble the LORD delivers him; the LORD protects him and keeps him alive; he is called blessed in the land; you do not give him up to the will of his enemies. The LORD sustains him on his sickbed; in his illness you restore him to full health.

PSALM 41:1-3, ESV

Who may worship in your sanctuary, LORD?
Who may enter your presence on your holy
hill? Those who lead blameless lives and
do what is right, speaking the truth from
sincere hearts. Those who refuse to gossip
or harm their neighbors or speak evil of
their friends. Those who despise flagrant
sinners, and honor the faithful followers of
the LORD, and keep their promises even when
it hurts.

PSALM 15:1-4

THE Lord IS MY FORTRESS;
my God is the mighty rock where I hide.

PSALM 94:22

Blessed are they
who observe justice,
who do righteousness
at all times!

PSALM 106:3, ESV

Sing to God, you kingdoms of the earth, sing praise to the Lord, to him who rides across the highest heavens, the ancient heavens, who thunders with mighty voice. Proclaim the power of God, whose majesty is over Israel, whose power is in the heavens. You, God, are awesome in your sanctuary; the God of Israel gives power and strength to his people. Praise be to God!

PSALM 68:32-35, NIV

The LORD is king! He is robed in majesty.
Indeed, the LORD is robed in majesty and
armed with strength. The world stands firm
and cannot be shaken. Your throne, O LORD,
has stood from time immemorial. You yourself
are from the everlasting past. . . . Your
royal laws cannot be changed. Your reign,
O LORD, is holy forever and ever.

PSALM 93:1-2, 5

Behold, God is my helper;

the Lord
is the upholder
of my life.

PSALM 54:4, ESV

Some trust in chariots, and some in horses: but we will

remember the
name of the
LORD
our God.

PSALM 20:7, KJV

O LORD, our Lord, your majestic name fills the earth! Your glory is higher than the heavens. . . . When I look at the night sky and see the work of your fingers—the moon and the stars you set in place—what are mere mortals that you should think about them, human beings that you should care for them?

PSALM 8:1, 3-4

The LORD has done great things for us, and we are filled with joy.

PSALM 126:3, NIV

Tell to the coming
generation the glorious
deeds of the LORD, and
his might, and the wonders
that he has done.

PSALM 78:4, ESV

Praise the LORD, all you who fear him! Honor him, all you descendants of Jacob! Show him reverence, all you descendants of Israel! For he has not ignored or belittled the suffering of the needy. He has not turned his back on them, but has listened to their cries for help. I will praise you in the great assembly.

PSALM 22:23-25

How lovely is your dwelling place, O Lord of Heaven's Armies. I long, yes, I faint with longing to enter the courts of the Lord. With my whole being, body and soul, I will shout joyfully to the living God. . . . What joy for those who can live in your house, always singing your praises.

PSALM 84:1-2, 4

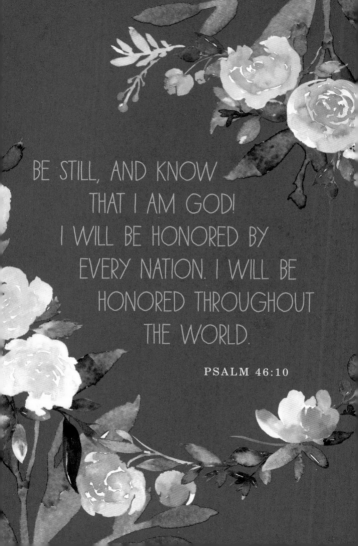

BE STILL, AND KNOW
THAT I AM GOD!
I WILL BE HONORED BY
EVERY NATION. I WILL BE
HONORED THROUGHOUT
THE WORLD.

PSALM 46:10

I AM TRUSTING YOU,
O Lord, SAYING,
"YOU ARE MY GOD!"

My future

IS IN YOUR HANDS.

PSALM 31:14-15

How wonderful and pleasant it is when brothers live together in harmony! For harmony is as precious as the anointing oil that was poured over Aaron's head, that ran down his beard and onto the border of his robe. Harmony is as refreshing as the dew from Mount Hermon that falls on the mountains of Zion. And there the LORD has pronounced his blessing, even life everlasting.

PSALM 133:1-3

The friendship of the LORD is for those who fear him, and he makes known to them his covenant. . . . Oh, guard my soul, and deliver me! Let me not be put to shame, for I take refuge in you.

PSALM 25:14, 20, ESV

YOU ARE MY STRENGTH;

I wait for you to rescue me, for you, O God, are my fortress.

PSALM 59:9

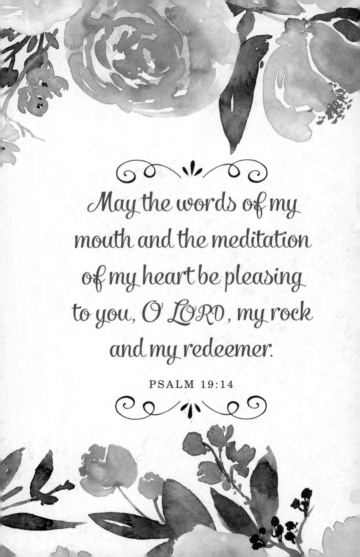

May the words of my mouth and the meditation of my heart be pleasing to you, O LORD, my rock and my redeemer.

PSALM 19:14

In my distress I prayed to the LORD, and the LORD answered me and set me free. . . . Yes, the LORD is for me; he will help me. . . . It is better to take refuge in the LORD than to trust in people. It is better to take refuge in the LORD than to trust in princes.

PSALM 118:5, 7-9

The LORD is king! Let the earth rejoice! Let the farthest coastlands be glad. . . . For you, O LORD, are supreme over all the earth; you are exalted far above all gods. . . . Light shines on the godly, and joy on those whose hearts are right. May all who are godly rejoice in the LORD and praise his holy name!

PSALM 97:1, 9, 11-12

Let the godly rejoice.
Let them be glad in God's presence.

Let them
be filled
with joy.

PSALM 68:3

Help me
understand
the meaning
of your
commandments,

and I will meditate on your wonderful deeds.

PSALM 119:27

Be still in the presence of the LORD, and wait patiently for him to act. Don't worry about evil people who prosper or fret about their wicked schemes. . . . Soon the wicked will disappear. Though you look for them, they will be gone. The lowly will possess the land and will live in peace and prosperity.

PSALM 37:7, 10-11

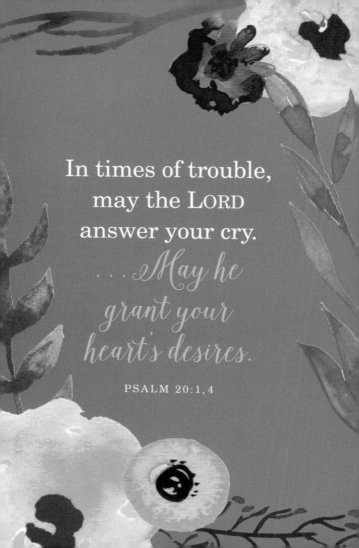

In times of trouble,
may the LORD
answer your cry.
...May he
grant your
heart's desires.

PSALM 20:1,4

Send out your
light and your truth;
let them guide me.
Let them lead me to your
holy mountain.

PSALM 43:3

The LORD is great, and greatly to be praised: he is to be feared above all gods. For all the gods of the nations are idols: but the LORD made the heavens. Honour and majesty are before him: strength and beauty are in his sanctuary.

PSALM 96:4-6, KJV

One generation shall praise Your works to another, and shall declare Your mighty acts. I will meditate on the glorious splendor of Your majesty, and on Your wondrous works. Men shall speak of the might of Your awesome acts, and I will declare Your greatness. They shall utter the memory of Your great goodness, and shall sing of Your righteousness.

PSALM 145:4-7, NKJV

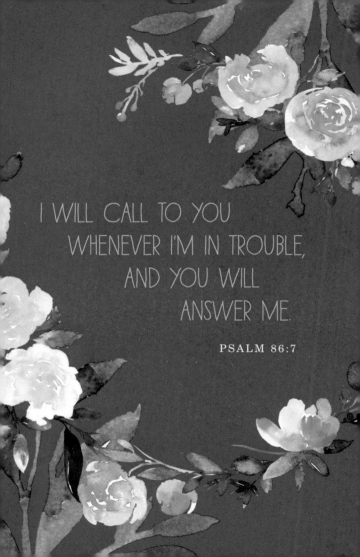

I WILL CALL TO YOU
WHENEVER I'M IN TROUBLE,
AND YOU WILL
ANSWER ME.

PSALM 86:7

EXALT THE Lord OUR GOD!
BOW LOW BEFORE

his feet,

FOR HE IS HOLY!

PSALM 99:5

Do not snatch your word of truth from me,
for your regulations are my only hope. I will
keep on obeying your instructions forever
and ever. I will walk in freedom, for I have
devoted myself to your commandments.

PSALM 119:43-45

I will praise You with my whole heart. . . .
I will worship toward Your holy temple, and
praise Your name for Your lovingkindness
and Your truth; for You have magnified Your
word above all Your name. In the day when
I cried out, You answered me, and made me
bold with strength in my soul.

PSALM 138:1-3, NKJV

THOUGH WE ARE OVERWHELMED BY OUR SINS,

you forgive them all.

PSALM 65:3

The LORD will give
justice to his people and
have compassion on
his servants.

PSALM 135:14

I will praise you, Lord, among the nations;
I will sing of you among the peoples. For
great is your love, reaching to the heavens;
your faithfulness reaches to the skies. Be
exalted, O God, above the heavens; let your
glory be over all the earth.

PSALM 57:9-11, NIV

He will not let you stumble; the one who watches over you will not slumber. Indeed, he who watches over Israel never slumbers or sleeps. The LORD himself watches over you! The LORD stands beside you as your protective shade. The sun will not harm you by day, nor the moon at night.

PSALM 121:3-6

Those who look to him for help
will be radiant with joy;

no shadow
of shame will
darken their
faces.

PSALM 34:5

Those
who love
your
instructions

have great peace and do not stumble.

PSALM 119:165

Give your love of justice to the king, O God, and righteousness to the king's son. Help him judge your people in the right way; let the poor always be treated fairly. May the mountains yield prosperity for all, and may the hills be fruitful. Help him to defend the poor, to rescue the children of the needy.

PSALM 72:1-4

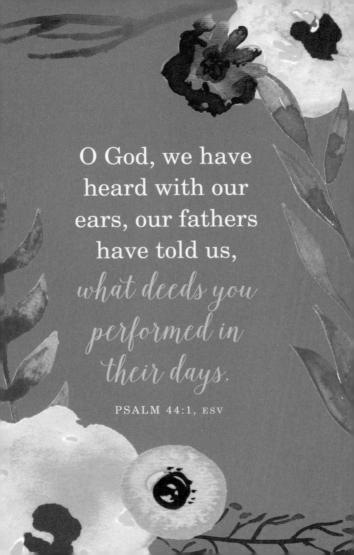

O God, we have heard with our ears, our fathers have told us, *what deeds you performed in their days.*

PSALM 44:1, ESV

Those who trust in
the LORD are like
Mount Zion, which
cannot be moved,
but abides forever.

PSALM 125:1, NKJV

Surely God is good to Israel, to those who are pure in heart. But as for me, my feet had almost slipped; I had nearly lost my foothold. . . . Yet I am always with you; you hold me by my right hand. You guide me with your counsel, and afterward you will take me into glory. Whom have I in heaven but you? And earth has nothing I desire besides you.

PSALM 73:1-2, 23-25, NIV

I cry out to the LORD; I plead for the
LORD's mercy. I pour out my complaints
before him and tell him all my troubles.
When I am overwhelmed, you alone know
the way I should turn. . . . I pray to you,
O LORD. I say, "You are my place of refuge.
You are all I really want in life."

PSALM 142:1-3, 5

THE LORD
REIGNS FOREVER. . . .
HE WILL JUDGE THE WORLD
WITH JUSTICE AND RULE THE
NATIONS WITH FAIRNESS.

PSALM 9:7-8

MAY THE LORD OUR GOD

show us

HIS APPROVAL AND MAKE
OUR EFFORTS SUCCESSFUL.

PSALM 90:17

Blessed is the one who trusts in the LORD, who does not look to the proud, to those who turn aside to false gods. Many, LORD my God, are the wonders you have done, the things you planned for us. None can compare with you; were I to speak and tell of your deeds, they would be too many to declare.

PSALM 40:4-5, NIV

Help us, O God of our salvation! Help us for the glory of your name. Save us and forgive our sins for the honor of your name. . . . Listen to the moaning of the prisoners. Demonstrate your great power by saving those condemned to die. . . . Then we your people, the sheep of your pasture, will thank you forever and ever, praising your greatness from generation to generation.

PSALM 79:9, 11, 13

GIVE THANKS TO THE
Lord AND PROCLAIM
HIS GREATNESS.
*Let the whole world
know what he has done.*

PSALM 105:1

The LORD's promises
are pure, like silver
refined in a furnace,
purified seven times over.

PSALM 12:6

Come quickly, LORD, and answer me, for my depression deepens. Don't turn away from me, or I will die. Let me hear of your unfailing love each morning, for I am trusting you. Show me where to walk, for I give myself to you. Rescue me from my enemies, LORD; I run to you to hide me.

PSALM 143:7-9

Come, bless the LORD, all you servants of
the LORD, who stand by night in the house
of the LORD! Lift up your hands to the holy
place and bless the LORD! May the LORD
bless you from Zion, he who made heaven
and earth!

PSALM 134:1-3, ESV

Praise the LORD,
for the LORD is good;

celebrate
his lovely name
with music.

PSALM 135:3

I will
exalt you,
LORD, for
you rescued me.
You refused

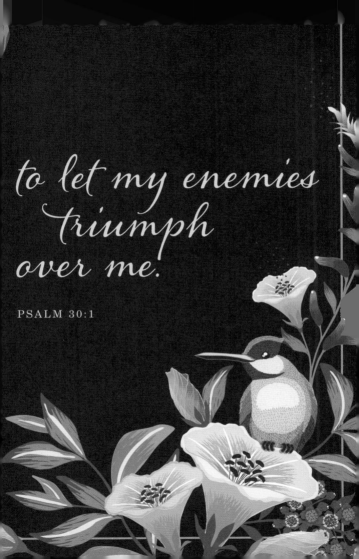

to let my enemies triumph over me.

PSALM 30:1

May God be merciful and bless us. May his face smile with favor on us. May your ways be known throughout the earth, your saving power among people everywhere. May the nations praise you, O God. Yes, may all the nations praise you.

PSALM 67:1-3

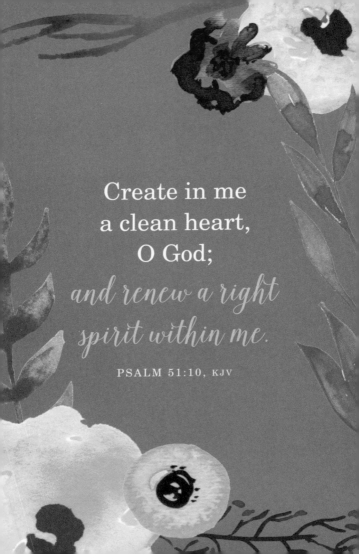

Create in me
a clean heart,
O God;
and renew a right
spirit within me.

PSALM 51:10, KJV

You, O LORD,
have made me glad
by your work; at the
works of your hands
I sing for joy.

PSALM 92:4, ESV

God is our refuge and strength, an ever-present help in trouble. Therefore we will not fear, though the earth give way and the mountains fall into the heart of the sea, though its waters roar and foam and the mountains quake with their surging.

PSALM 46:1-3, NIV

The LORD, the Mighty One, is God, and he has spoken; he has summoned all humanity from where the sun rises to where it sets. From Mount Zion, the perfection of beauty, God shines in glorious radiance. Our God approaches, and he is not silent. Fire devours everything in his way, and a great storm rages around him. He calls on the heavens above and earth below to witness the judgment of his people.

PSALM 50:1-4

I TAKE JOY IN DOING
YOUR WILL, MY GOD,
FOR YOUR INSTRUCTIONS
ARE WRITTEN
ON MY HEART.

PSALM 40:8

I HAVE CHOSEN THE WAY
OF FAITHFULNESS; I HAVE SET

my heart

ON YOUR LAWS. I HOLD FAST
TO YOUR STATUTES, LORD.

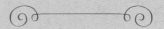

PSALM 119:30-31, NIV

I will praise the LORD at all times. I will
constantly speak his praises. I will boast
only in the LORD; let all who are helpless
take heart. Come, let us tell of the LORD's
greatness; let us exalt his name together.

PSALM 34:1-3

Give thanks to the LORD, for he is good! His faithful love endures forever. Has the LORD redeemed you? Then speak out! Tell others he has redeemed you from your enemies. For he has gathered the exiles from many lands. . . . Let them praise the LORD for his great love and for the wonderful things he has done for them.

PSALM 107:1-3, 8

I WILL PRAISE YOU, Lord, WITH ALL MY HEART;

I will tell of all the marvelous things you have done.

PSALM 9:1

I lift my eyes to you,
O God, enthroned
in heaven.

PSALM 123:1

Let my cry come before you, O LORD; give
me understanding according to your word!
. . . My lips will pour forth praise, for you
teach me your statutes. . . . I long for your
salvation, O LORD, and your law is my delight.
Let my soul live and praise you, and let
your rules help me. I have gone astray like
a lost sheep; seek your servant, for I do
not forget your commandments.

PSALM 119:169, 171, 174–176, ESV

LIVING EXPRESSIONS COLLECTION

Living Expressions invites you to explore God's Word
and express your creativity in ways that are refreshing
to the spirit and restorative to the soul.

Visit Tyndale online at www.tyndale.com.

TYNDALE, Tyndale's quill logo, *Living Expressions*, and the Living Expressions
logo are registered trademarks of Tyndale House Publishers, Inc.

A Bouquet of Favorite Psalms to Inspire Your Soul

For information about special discounts for bulk purchases, please contact
Tyndale House Publishers at csresponse@tyndale.com, or call 1-800-323-9400.

ISBN 978-1-4964-3605-4

Printed in China

24	23	22	21	20	19	18
7	6	5	4	3	2	1